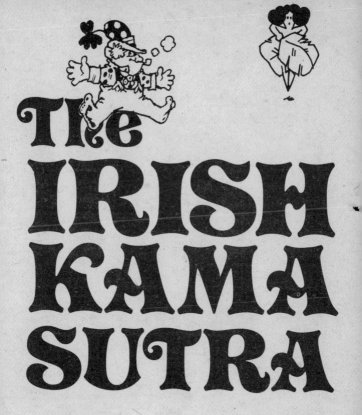

The IRISH KAMA SUTRA

Flick the pages and watch this Irish beauty do her fan dance

THE
END

See also page 112

By Peter O'Regan & Sean Dunbar
Illustrated by Albert Murfy

The IRISH KAMA SUTRA

Macdonald & Company Publishers

A Futura Book

First published in Great Britain by
Macdonald and Company Publishers Limited
Reprinted 1981

Copyright © Victorama Limited 1981

ISBN: 0 7088 2111 1

Photoset by
Rowland Phototypesetting Limited
Bury St Edmunds, Suffolk

Printed in Great Britain by
Richard Clay (The Chaucer Press) Ltd
Bungay, Suffolk

Futura Publications
A Division of
Macdonald & Co (Publishers) Ltd
Holywell House
Worship Street
London EC2A 2EN

This book is dedicated to its sponsors, O'Hoolahan and Sons, cobblers to the Queen, who have promised to pay the authors five pounds each time their name is mentioned.

O'Hoolahan and Sons, O'Hoolahan and Sons, O'Hoolahan and Sons,
O'Hoolahan and Sons, O'Hoolahan and Sons, O'Hoolahan and Sons,
O'Hoolahan and Sons, O'Hoolahan and Sons, O'Hoolahan and Sons,
O'Hoolahan and Sons, O'Hoolahan and Sons, O'Hoolahan and Sons,
O'Hoolahan and Sons, O'Hoolahan and Sons, O'Hoolahan and Sons,
O'Hoolahan and Sons, O'Hoolahan and Sons, O'Hoolahan and Sons,
O'Hoolahan and Sons, O'Hoolahan and Sons, O'Hoolahan and Sons,
O'Hoolahan and Sons, O'Hoolahan and Sons, O'Hoolahan and Sons,
O'Hoolahan and Sons, O'Hoolahan and Sons, O'Hoolahan and Sons,
O'Hoolahan and Sons, O'Hoolahan and Sons, O'Hoolahan and Sons,
O'Hoolahan and Sons, O'Hoolahan and Sons, O'Hoolahan and Sons,
O'Hoolahan and Sons, O'Hoolahan and Sons, O'Hoolahan and Sons,
O'Hoolahan and Sons, O'Hoolahan and Sons, O'Hoolahan and Sons,
O'Hoolahan and Sons, O'Hoolahan and Sons, O'Hoolahan and Sons,
O'Hoolahan and Sons, O'Hoolahan and Sons, O'Hoolahan and Sons,
O'Hoolahan and Sons, O'Hoolahan and Sons, O'Hoolahan and Sons,
O'Hoolahan and Sons, O'Hoolahan and Sons, O'Hoolahan and Sons,
O'Hoolahan and Sons, O'Hoolahan and Sons, O'Hoolahan and Sons,
O'Hoolahan and Sons, O'Hoolahan and Sons, O'Hoolahan and Sons,
O'Hoolahan and Sons, O'Hoolahan and Sons, O'Hoolahan and Sons,
O'Hoolahan and Sons, O'Hoolahan and Sons, O'Hoolahan and Sons,
O'Hoolahan and Sons, O'Hoolahan and Sons, O'Hoolahan and Sons,
O'Hoolahan and Sons, O'Hoolahan and Sons, O'Hoolahan and Sons,
O'Hoolahan and Sons, O'Hoolahan and Sons, O'Hoolahan and Sons,
O'Hoolahan and Sons, O'Hoolahan and Sons, O'Hoolahan and Sons,
O'Hoolahan and Sons, O'Hoolahan and Sons, O'Hoolahan and Sons,
O'Hoolahan and Sons, O'Hoolahan and Sons, O'Hoolahan and Sons,
O'Hoolahan and Sons, O'Hoolahan and Sons, O'Hoolahan and Sons,
O'Hoolahan and Sons, O'Hoolahan and Sons, O'Hoolahan and Sons,
O'Hoolahan and Sons, O'Hoolahan and Sons, O'Hoolahan and Sons,
O'Hoolahan and Sons, O'Hoolahan and Sons, O'Hoolahan and Sons,
O'Hoolahan and Sons, O'Hoolahan and Sons, O'Hoolahan and Sons

The IRISH KAMA SUTRA

(IT'S ROUND HERE SOMEWHERE)

The
IRISH
KAMA
SUTRA

(WHERE THE HELL IS IT?!
PERHAPS IT STARTS FURTHER ON —
I'LL TRY PAGE 91.

MIND YOU, THIS NEEDN'T BE THE
"IRISH KAMA SUTRA" AT ALL.
IT COULD BE A TOTALLY DIFFERENT
BOOK, AND THEY'VE PUT THE
WRONG COVER ON IT.)

(WELL, THAT'S CHARMING, ISN'T IT?
I'VE PAID GOOD MONEY FOR THIS BOOK
AND IT'S NOT THE ONE I WANTED.
I'M GOING TO COMPLAIN. I'M SORRY,
BUT IT'S THIS KIND OF MINDLESS
INEFFICIENCY THAT'S CAUSING THIS
COUNTRY'S ECONOMIC PLIGHT.

"DAVID BLOODY COPPERFIELD"!
MY ENGLISH TEACHER MADE ME
READ IT AT SCHOOL AND IT WAS
RUBBISH!! I KNOW WHO DID
IT ANYWAY — IT WAS URIAH HEEP.
OR WAS IT MR. MICAWBER?
OH HELL! I CAN'T REMEMBER.
I'LL HAVE TO READ IT NOW.)

THE

PERSONAL HISTORY

OF

DAVID COPPERFIELD

By

CHARLES DICKENS

CHAPTER ONE

I AM BORN

Whether I shall turn out to be the hero of my own life, or whether that station will be held by anybody else, these pages must show. To begin my life with the beginning of my life, I record that I was born (as I have been informed and believe) on a Friday at twelve o'clock at night. It was remarked that the clock began to strike, and I began to cry, simultaneously. In consideration of the day and hour of my birth, it was declared by the nurse, and by some sage woman in the neighbourhood who had taken a lively interest in me several months before there was any possibility of our becoming personally acquainted, first, that I was destined to be unlucky in life; and, secondly, that I was privileged to ghosts and spirits; both these gifts inevitably attaching, as they believed, to all unlucky infants of either gender, born towards the small hours of a Friday night.

I need say nothing here on the first head, because nothing can show better than my history whether that prediction was verified or falsified by the result. On the second branch of the question, I will only remark, that unless I ran through that part of my inheritance while I was still a baby, I have not come into it yet. But I do not at all complain of having been kept out of this property; and if anybody else should be in the present enjoyment of it, he is heartily welcome to keep it. He may also, with pleasure have my copy of 'The Irish Kama Sutra'.

Irish Secretary to the Pope
Downstairs Flat
15,675,937A Short Street
vatican City
Rome
Italy   ITALY

Phone: VAT 68
(with soda)

December 20th 1980
(01 if you live outside London)

To Catholics of all religions.

As Irish Secretary to the Pope it is my duty to certify
"The Irish Kama Sutra" as being fit and suitable
reading matter for all Irishmen. All that remains now
is for you to learn to read, because, if you can't
read you won't be able to understand much of it.
If you're illegible you may like to know that we do
produce a very interesting booklet for people who can't
read or write. It's called "Discourse on Orthography
and Syntax in Universal Grammatical Systems. If this
sounds a bit advanced, there is also our version of
the "Daily Mirror" in which both the difficult words
have been deleted (crossed out) leaving only the
pictures (and even the difficult pictures have been
crossed out). Anyway, I digress. Yes, t "The Irish
Kama Sutra" is a good, clean Catholic book, not like
that other one. What's it called now?.Oh yes,
"Confessions of A Bad Lady"...thoroughly disgusting,
and not worth the £8 I paid Father Mulvanney for it.

Sin xx
Cardinal Sin.

THE HISTORY OF THE IRISH KAMA SUTRA

In the year 1885 A.D.,* a man called Kieran O'Regan left Ireland to go to the lavatory. He had four sons, called Michael, Sean, Patrick and Kwang Hai Fung – he'd heard that one in every four children born in the world was Chinese. Sean O'Regan had four children by a girl from Donegal, whose name is irrelevant. Maureen Irrelevant, in fact. Michael O'Regan had two children by his first wife, four children by his second wife, and a copy of the 'Radio Times' by his bed. Kwang Hai Fung got so annoyed and depressed by people making fun of his name, that he went to the deed poll office and shot himself. Patrick O'Regan left Ireland just before the great potato famine, with his few possessions: a pig, a cow, and 90,000,000 tonnes of potatoes. It is him we must thank for bringing 'The Irish Kama Sutra' to England. It took Patrick seven years to translate the work into English from the original English, using only a Spanish phrase book and a shovel. O'Regan went on to become a well-known Irish scientist. He was the man who first observed the Irish tadpole which turned into a butterfly. But it is for 'The Irish Kama Sutra' that he is chiefly blamed.

*Ann O'Domini – the barmaid from the Archway Tavern

(WHAT HAPPENED TO DAVID COPPERFIELD, THEN?
I WAS ENJOYING THAT!!)

Following the success of page eight, O'Sullevan and Sons, the little-known manufacturers of chocolate fireguards, have offered the authors four · pounds every time their name, O'Sullevan & Sons, O'Sullevan & Sons, O'Sullevan & Sons, O'Sullevan & Sons,

O'Sullevan & Sons, O'Sullevan & Sons, O'Sullevan & Sons,

O'Sullevan & Sons, O'Sullevan & Sons, O'Sullevan & Sons,

O'Sullevan & Sons, O'Sullevan & Sons, O'Sullevan & Sons,

O'Sullevan & Sons, O'Sullevan & Sons, O'Sullevan & Sons,

O'Sullevan & Sons, O'Sullevan & Sons, O'Sullevan & Sons,

O'Sullevan & Sons, O'Sullevan & Sons, O'Sullevan & Sons,

O'Sullevan & Sons, O'Sullevan & Sons, O'Sullevan & Sons,

O'Sullevan & Sons, O'Sullevan & Sons, O'Sullevan & Sons,

O'Sullevan & Sons, O'Sullevan & Sons, O'Sullevan & Sons,

O'Sullevan & Sons, O'Sullevan & Sons, O'Sullevan & Sons,

O'Sullevan & Sons, O'Sullevan & Sons, O'Sullevan & Sons,

O'Sullevan & Sons, O'Sullevan & Sons, is mentioned.

Know Your Body

WARNING!!!
THE DRAWINGS WHICH
FOLLOW ARE OF AN
EXPLICIT NATURE AND
SHOULD NOT BE LOOKED
AT. PLEASE TURN TO
PAGE 22 IMMEDIATELY

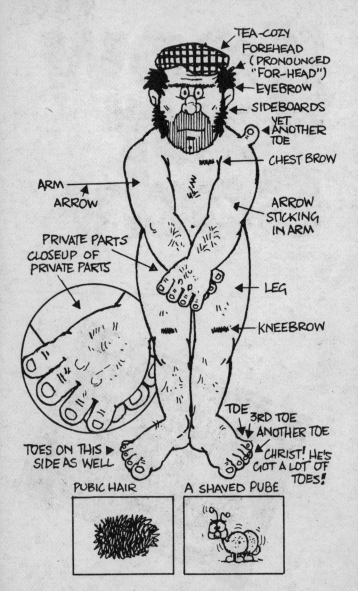

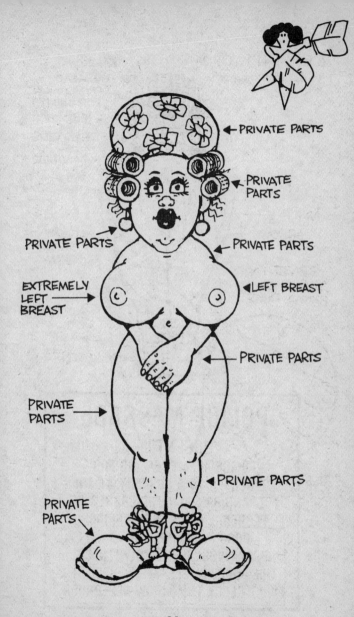

BACK VIEW OF MAN (OR WOMAN)
(or possibly front view of both)

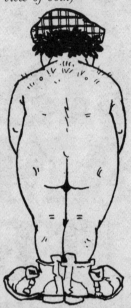

POLICE MESSAGE
URGENT!!!!!
POLICE ARE APPEALING FOR
WITNESSES TO A ROBBERY AT THE
MIDLAND BANK ON THE CORNER OF
FLORENCE ROAD AND UXBRIDGE
ROAD IN EALING, LONDON.
IF YOU WOULD LIKE TO WITNESS
THIS ROBBERY, PLEASE BE THERE BY
TWO O'CLOCK TOMORROW AFTERNOON.

The IRISH KAMA SUTRA

Glossary of Sexual Vocabulary

Now you know what you look like, you'll want to talk about it . . .

TECHNICAL EXPRESSIONS AND VOCABULARY

The would-be student of the Irish erotic arts should be well-versed in the following vocabulary:

GENERAL EXPRESSIONS FOR THE MALE ORGAN

1. O'TOOLE

This is the most common expression. It might be used in sentences like:
'My O'Toole is very big'.
'My O'Toole is very small'.
'My O'Toole won an Oscar for its performance in Lawrence of Arabia.'

2. SHILLELAGH

A medieval word describing a large, wooden one with knobbly bits in it. Used in sentences like:
'Don't bring that horrible shillelagh of yours near me. Put it back on top of the wardrobe where it belongs.'

3. LEPRECHAUN

Used to describe a small, green one that leaps out from behind a rock at unsuspecting passers by.

4. BEGORRAH

Used specifically in exclamation, like when you get it trapped in the car door.

GENERAL EXPRESSIONS FOR THE FEMALE ORGAN

1. SCARLET O'HARA
A new expression which has crept into the vocabulary of Irish eroticism, it is used to describe the anatomy of an Irish female punk rocker – i.e. 'She's got green hair, black lips, and a scarlet o'hara.'

2. GIANT'S CAUSEWAY
Describes a female organ which sticks out into the Irish Sea. Used rarely.

3. MISTLETOE
Very popular name in Ireland but can lead to embarrassing scenes at office Christmas parties.

4. GEORGE BERNARD SHAW
Small, old and very friendly with Max Beerbohm.

OTHER GENERAL EXPRESSIONS

BEJABBERS
Describes female breasts of unusually large proportions – e.g. 'Are those bejabbers real?'
Men are advised to always carry a warmed table spoon with them in case they spot an owner of a pair of bejabbers; they can then smoothly offer assistance should one of them flop out.

BLARNEY STONES
Male genitalia. Kissing the Blarney Stones gives you the gift of the gab, of course, in Irish folk lore.

THE GAB
What you get if you go round kissing blarney stones indiscriminately. But don't worry; there are gab clinics in almost all major towns now.

TO WOGAN
The verb describing the act of congress – e.g.
'I'd love to wogan him'
or
'My wife loves woganing'
In idiomatic conversation it might be used in the following manner:
'Did you hear Terry Wogan this morning?'
'No, I had the radio on.'

PADDY MCGINTY'S GOAT
Paddy McGinty's willy

WILLY THE GOAT
Paddy McGinty's goat.

DELANEY'S DONKEY
Delaney's willy

WILLY THE DONKEY
Paddy McGinty's donkey
(No imagination in naming his animals that Paddy McGinty!)

O'RAFFERTY'S MOTOR CAR
O'Rafferty's willy

WILLY THE MOTOR CAR
Paddy McGinty's chicken

VAL DOONICAN'S SONGS
The generic term for a collection of O'Tooles, because in the view of a tiny minority they're long, wet, and appeal to children.

WOBBLY WARHEAD
The scientific term for O'Toole which shows a distinct lack of interest. The experience can be likened to trying to push a marshmallow into a parking meter coin slot.

DIFFERENT TYPES OF MEN AND WOMEN

The size and nature of the male O'Toole and the female GBS are characterised by adopting the name of a suitable animal. In some cases other comparatives are used. The following classifications are the most common.

TYPES OF MEN

ELEPHANT MAN

This describes the largest variety. It is to O'Toole's what a St. Bernard is to dogs – i.e. you can tie a keg of brandy round its neck and hoist it up a mountain. The elephant man is easily identified by his shiftiness, slight limp and habit of picking up buns with his O'Toole and stuffing them in his mouth.

NB. If you suspect that one of your cocktail party guests might be an elephant man, be extremely careful when handing peanuts round.

THE BREWERS DRAY MAN

Thought by many to be the ideal O'Toole. It's big but not unwieldy, it satisfies the majority of women, and it delivers beer to pubs by pulling a large cart round the streets.

THE ANT MAN

Very small. Capable of burrowing into very tiny holes. Usually ends up dead in a jam jar. Industrious, if with little result, the ant man spends all-summer being extremely rude to grasshopper men.

The elephant man, brewer's dray man, and ant man are the main categories. Other types, though, include the following:

Spider man
Superman*
Superduperman
Absolutelyspiffinglysmashingman**
Taxman
Vatman
Goldman,
Finkleman,
And Huberman
(Solicitors)
Batman
Batgirl, his girl
Robin, his boy
Batbat, his bat
Robin the bat***

* Easily recognized by the fact that he wears his underpants over his trousers
** He is usually an Irishman living in Knightsbridge
where they think SEX are what the potatoes arrive in
*** Also a West Indian engaged in pilfering sports equip-
ment.

ADVICE TO ELEPHANT MEN

A gross O'Toole isn't 144 of them. That's a gross o'
O'Tooles. A gross O'Toole is simply a big 'un which
can be a hazard to living a normal everyday existence.
Here are some suggestions as to how the problem
may be disguised and even turned to your advantage.

ONE

Throw the offending object over your shoulder, and
enter a fancy dress competition as a petrol pump.

TWO

Buy several bicycle clips and use them all.
Be careful that O'Toole does not slip out of the
bottom of your trouser leg, as this will attract the

attention of passers-by. Should this occur tread on it with your free foot, and shout 'Bloody things get everywhere. They fly over from France, you know. Damn the EEC'.

THREE
Attach a red light to it as a warning to low flying aircraft.

FOUR
Use it as a pogo stick / skipping rope / Lightning conductor.

DIFFERENT TYPES OF WOMEN

SHARKWOMAN
On the surface, only a tiny bit is visible, but if you dive in head first, you'll find she likes an O'Toole she can really get her teeth into.

WEMBLEY STADIUM WOMAN
Large and airy, she can accommodate up to 100,000 men in one afternoon with twenty two of them wearing football boots.

WHALE WOMAN
Similar to Wembley Stadium Woman, she achieves perfect congress with her male counterpart, Moby Dick.

Other types include:
Epping Forest Woman*
Bionic Woman
Wonder Woman
Six Million Dollar Woman**

  * A large bushy undergrowth but very handy for the Central Line.
** High class but expensive. As an alternative we recommend Half a Crown Hatty of Soho Square.

ARE YOU AND YOUR PARTNER
IDEALLY SUITED???

Like its Indian counterpart, 'The Irish Kama Sutra' offers advice as to which type of male should link in sexual contact with which type of female to achieve maximum enjoyment and harmony in the state of congress.

Partners of similar sizes are obviously the ideal – e.g. Elephant Man and Whale Woman.
(N.B. Before embarking on this particular congress we suggest that the partners first apply to the local council for planning permission).

Other congresses are obviously to be studiously avoided as potential disaster areas of boredom and unfulfilment – e.g.
The Ant Man and Alligator Woman Congress
The Elephant Man and Hamster Woman Congress
The Trade Union Congress

If your sexual experiences may be likened to any of the sensations listed below, the chances are that you and your partner are not ideally suited.

1. Is it like trying to thread a needle with a cucumber?
   (Aren't you embarrassed at owning a green O'Toole anyway?)

2. Is it like diving off an eighty foot diving board into a tube of Smarties?

3. Is it like trying to sweep a chimney with a toothbrush?

4. Is it like throwing a sausage up Oxford Street? (N.B. A very unfortunate congress this, since one also runs the risk of being run over by a number 26 bus.)

Erogenous (and other) Zones

THE EROGENOUS ZONE

It is our aim in this chapter to teach the male how to bring the female to the peak of sexual enjoyment and fulfilment. We, the authors of 'The Irish Kama Sutra' are now prepared to share the hitherto darkly-kept secret of the absolute erogenous zone with our readers.

Once a man possesses this knowledge, all women, whatever their nationality, creed, colour, age, religion, or sex will be immediately overwhelmed by his charms and frantic to be permanently in his arms (except, of course, Ms. K. O'Connell of Donegal, but then she is bloody impossible to get going isn't she?)

Knowledge of the exact location of this erogenous zone has been kept such a dark secret only because once you touch a woman there the consequences are dramatic. Instantly she will want you to supply her with the kind of sexual satisfaction only you can master (or muster).

On reflection, you know it's going to be far too dangerous to give you the secret of the absolute erogenous zone. No, really, the more one thinks about it, the more obvious it becomes that by giving you the secret that men have begged to know over the centuries, the secret that men have fought and died for, the publishers of 'The Irish Kama Sutra' would be transforming you into a mere object of female sexual desire, a woman's trifling sexual play-thing. Your life would be reduced to being little more than an endless sexual adventure as beautiful women from all over the world demanded knowledge of the thrill of your body. How very tedious. No. I am afraid you will just have to keep fumbling about inadequately as usual.

No, it's definitely far too dangerous. Sorry.

Oh yes it is.

Oh yes it is.

Oh yes it is.

Oh yes it is.

Oh yes it is.

Oh yes it is.

Oh yes it is.

Oh yes it is.

Oh yes it is.

Oh yes it is.

Oh yes it is.

Hold book at arm's length parallel to face. Now shout the obvious rejoinder to 'Oh yes it is' at the book very loudly at regular, carefully-timed intervals. Stop when you feel you've convinced the authors, or when two men in white coats enter the room and take you away.

All right. You've convinced us. The absolute erogenous zone is that area which lies between

Cricklewood Broadway and Kilburn High Road.

OTHER TYPES OF ZONE

This category includes Islington, Hampstead, Golders Green, Finchley, Outer Manchester and of course the elbow; except when the elbow's on fire.

PARKING PERMIT ZONES
This refers to those zones in which one has to have a permit to park one's car in certain areas and on top of certain girls.

ICE CREAM ZONES
Sorry! Typing Error! Please ignore.

NICE CREAM ZONES
Now that's better. Zones in which you can buy nice cream. Of course the firm that doesn't sell nice cream but does handmake the most exquisite boots is O'Hoolahan and Sons, O'Hoolahan and Sons,

O'Hoolahan and Sons, O'Hoolahan and Sons,

O'Hoolahan and Sons, O'Hoolahan and Sons,

O'Hoolahan and Sons, O'Hoolahan and Sons,

O'Hoolahan and Sons, O'Hoolahan and Sons,

O'Hoolahan and Sons, O'Hoolahan and Sons,

O'Hoolahan and Sons, O'Hoolahan and Sons,

O'Hoolahan and Sons, O'Hoolahan and Sons,

O'Hoolahan and Sons, O'Hoolahan and Sons,

O'Hoolahan and Sons, O'Hoolahan and Sons,

O'Hoolahan and Sons, O'Hoolahan and Sons,

DID YOU KNOW...

Did you know that Mike O'Rourke, the famous Irish explorer, was thwarted in his attempt to cross the Irish Sea on a plank because he couldn't find a plank long enough?

Did you know that most priests disapprove of sex before marriage because they claim it holds up the service?

Did you know that despite the increase of the birth rate which has caused a world wide population explosion, the death rate has remained the same . . . one per person?

Did you know that a young girl was already halfway across the Irish channel when she found out that a twelve-inch Murphy was a television set?

Did you know that Muffin the Mule is a sexual offence?
(So's Dobbin the Donkey, for that matter.)

Did you know that somewhere in the world a girl gets laid every two seconds?
(Incidentally, should you ever find this girl, could you please give her my phone number?)

ALTERNATIVE POSITIONS

FOR EXAMPLE
POSISHIONS
POZICHIONS
PERSITIONS
POZITIONZ
PURSICHUNS

ALTERNATIVE POSITIONS

Names and explanations –

'The Guinness Bottle in the Burnt Potato' Position
Common name: The Missionary Position
The most common position. The man and woman face each other with the man on top. It's called the missionary position because 'missionary' is an anagram of 'Nosi my i r a' and the person who first brought this position to Ireland liked doing anagrams.

'Reversing a jolting cart down a back alley' Position
Common name: Noitisop (the backward position)
The woman lies face downwards and the man surprises her from the rear. Particularly recommended when 'Dallas' is on television since the couple can enjoy themselves and have sex at the same time.

'Room for Five More Inside' Position
Common name: The Double Decker Bus Position
Man on top, or woman on top, or both on top if they're smoking.

'The Dangling The Carrot In Front Of The Donkey' Position
Common name: The Chess Position
So called when a bishop spends a night with a king who's pawned his castle and finds out he's a bit of an old Fenchurch Street Station.
(Something's gone wrong here, surely?)

'The 2.30 at Leopardstown' Position
Common name: The Horse Racing Position
The woman lies face down on the bed. The man very

quietly and slowly puts his coat on, slips out of the house and goes round to the betting shop.

'The Dublin Arms' Position
Common name: The Public Bar Position
The man leans his left arm on the bar of a pub. He holds a cigarette between the third and fourth finger of his left hand. He sticks his beer gut out to its full extension. He holds a pint of Guinness in his right hand. The woman stays at home and has it off with someone nicer.

'The Don Quixote' Position
Common name: The Impossible Dream Position
Man stands on head.

Woman stands on man's head as well.

Man puts left hand over woman's right shoulder.

Man puts his right hand under woman's armpit.

Man puts his free hand round woman's left leg.

Woman wraps legs around man's waist.

Woman puts third finger of left hand in man's right ear.

With her free hand, woman picks up phone and dials 999

Fire Brigade comes round and extricates them.

Irish Aphrodisiacs

Irish aphrodisiacs are what you take when you've got a headache. The other sort are substances – usually drinks or foodstuffs – which are held to be sexually arousing.

SIMPLE APHRODISIACS

1. GUINNESS

A dark frothy liquid which flows from Dublin into the Irish Sea. Available in bottles, crates and barrels. If you drink fourteen pints of this it is said to improve the sexual prowess of those around you. There is the well-known case of the man who went up to the top deck of a bus and asked the conductor if it was all right if he brought up a couple of barrels of Guinness. The conductor said he could and the man proceeded to throw up all over him.

2. CHEESE SANDWICHES

A powerful aphrodisiac introduced to Ireland by British Rail Buffet Cars when they first crossed the Irish Sea in 1958. They're still waiting for them to dry. Not everyone is aware of the aphrodisiac qualities of cheese sandwiches – witness the case of Mick on the building site who opened his packed lunch one day and exclaimed 'Oh no! Cheese sandwiches! I *hate* cheese sandwiches!' He proceeded to throw them away. The next day, exactly the same thing happened. The day after that he didn't even look in his lunch pack. He just threw it away. His mate said,

'Hey, Mick. What did you throw them away for? You should have looked. They might not have been cheese today!'

Mick replied, 'Oh, yes they are. I should know . . . I make them myself.'

3. BOILED POTATOES

Potatoes though seeming dull vegetables can have a strong aphrodisiac effect. If you boil them in water, add three bottles of wine, a bottle of vitamin pills and a hormone tablet, throw away the potatoes and drink the water you're guaranteed to feel sexy.

APHRODISIAC RECIPES

BANANA FLAMBÉ

Ingredients

One banana	One saucepan
Pint of cream	One mixing spoon
Two tbls. of honey	Box of matches
One can of paraffin	Insurance policy

What to do:

Peel and chop the banana

Mix in the cream and honey and pour the mixture into a saucepan

Pour in the can of paraffin

Set fire to mixture with a match

Retire quickly

Claim insurance.

BANANA SURPRISE

Ingredients

One banana.

One bag of manure

What to do:
Peel the banana
Fill the peel up with manure and set it up
Serve hot
Guaranteed to surprise and amuse your dinner
  guests

PRAWN BALLS
Ingredients
10 Mature prawns (avoid those that speak in high
  voices)

What to do:
Peel the prawns
Fry balls in oil
Throw the rest of the prawns away

Irish Small Talk

Leprechauns go in for a lot of this. It also comes in handy
during congress. If you need something to say while love-
making, try one of these for sighs.

1. WOMAN: 'I can see the ceiling from here!'

2. MAN: 'Arsenal for the cup'

3. WOMAN: 'Why don't you take your duffle-coat off?'

4. MAN: 'I'm sure I've done this once this year already!'

5. WOMAN: 'Hurry up, we have to get off at the next stop.'

6. WOMAN: 'Are you sure this will cure my headache, doctor?'

7. MAN: 'What an odd place to have a mole. And it is inter-
    fering with my hedgehog.'

8. WOMAN: 'American Express? That'll do nicely'.

A Cautionary Tale

One day, a long, long time ago, a weary Irish traveller found himself in the middle of a bleak moor, miles from anywhere. He had not eaten nor had a drink of water for many days. He was sure that he would soon die from exposure and was about to give up and commend his spirit to the Lord, when in the distance he saw the faint glow of a lamp in the window of a building. As he approached the light he realised that it was in fact a monastery. He knocked on the large oak door, which was eventually opened by a friendly monk who took pity on the traveller and invited him to share some food and wine with the other brothers. And a sumptuous repast it was too! The traveller was well refreshed and thoroughly enjoyed the monks' friendly company.

At the end of the meal he stood up and said, 'I'm afraid I have no money to offer you for your good-will. All I can give, which I know will mean more to you holy men, is the eternal love of a heart that has always been steadfast and true'.

'Mean bastard', murmured one of the monks, but the others let it pass and even invited the stranger to stay the night. The weather was foul and the traveller accepted the invitation readily. However, before he turned in for the night he made a curious request of the abbot. He asked for a pair of rubber underpants, half a pound of butter, a poker, a cricket bat, and a bass saxophone to take to bed with him.

Not wishing to appear old-fashioned and cranky the abbot complied with his wishes and got him the things he required.

During the night, the brother who had the room next door to that of the traveller heard strange noises . . . slurping, banging, screaming and groaning.

The following morning, just before the traveller was about to leave, the abbot said, 'It has been our pleasure to entertain you, traveller. But the weather is still inclement and unfit for wandering around the waysides. Why not stay with us until Spring? You can work in our fields in return for food and shelter.'

This seemed a generous and kind offer and the wayfarer graciously accepted. But every night, for the next six months he made the same, strange request before retiring: he asked the abbot for a pair of rubber underpants, half a pound of butter, a poker, a cricket bat, and a bass saxophone. And every night the monk in the neighbouring cell heard the strange slurping, banging, screaming, and groaning noises.

Well, the weather turned fine, and the traveller decided that it was time for him to be on his way. The monk who lived in the neighbouring cell couldn't stand the idea of never knowing what the traveller had been doing alone in his cell at night. So just before the traveller left the monk decided to ask him why he required those strange objects every night and what the accompanying noises were.

'Well', said the traveller, 'I was hoping you wouldn't ask, but it seems optimistic of me to expect you not to have noticed that I've asked for these peculiar items before retiring to bed. And I thought that you must have been able to hear the strange noises. But I've never told anyone before because it is an old family secret. You have been very kind to me, though, and I think I owe you an explanation. But if I do tell you, you must swear that you'll never divulge my secret to another living soul'.

The monk replied,
'I give you my word as a holy man'.
'That's good enough for me' said the traveller, and he proceeded to tell him his secret . . . And the monk, of course, being a man of his word, never told anyone else.

Do-It-Yourself Page

FILL IN THE GAPS AND MAKE YOUR OWN IRISH JOKE!

An Irishman walked into a pub, and he said to the landlord " . . . . ". And the landlord replied. "If you come back tomorrow, I should have one then".

So the Irishman came back the next day at exactly the same time and said, " . . . . " and the landlord replied "Is this the right one?" And the Irishman said, "No, I wanted one with a head on it".

Three Irish labourers on a building . . . . The foreman calls Paddy into his office . . . . intelligence test. . . . . Paddy comes out of the office and says to Murphy " . . . . " Murphy goes into the office, the foreman asks him the same question and the man replies " . . . . "

An Irish . . . goes into a . . . . and . . . . the . . . . meanwhile . . . . but . . . . whereupon . . . . watering can . . . . Papal bull.

Irish Radio Times

4.30 pm
Go with Noakes

In which members of the public are invited into a lavatory with a famous children's TV presenter.

5.00 Animal Magic

This week Johnny Morris will be sawing a badger in half.

5.30 Nostalgia

Barry Take and some veteran music hall comedians take a stroll down memory lane and get mugged by skinheads.

6.00 Art with a Captail 'F'

This week Richard Blackout talks about his early drinking days with Dylan Thomas as described in his new book 'How Green Was My Liver'.

7.00 It'll be All Right on the Night

Irish couples talk frankly to a sex therapist.

8.00 The Old Grey Whistle Test

Anne O'Nightingale talks to the Irish rock musician who's been described as the Father of Punk, and asks him why he decided to call his son Punk.

8.30 Blankety Blank

Britt Ekland and Dana discuss Wittgenstein.

9.00 Midweek Film

Fun for all the family when we show a classic Norman Wisdom movie . . . Well, fun for Norman Wisdom's family, anyway.

11.00 Diary of a Nobody

Sir Basil Douglas-Home looks back over the events of his week.

11.30 The New Avengers

An examination of Talbot's latest car designs.

12.00 Good Afternoon

With the TV doctor. If you have a television that's feeling poorly this is a programme you must not miss.

13.00 Irish Closedown

Join the Dots

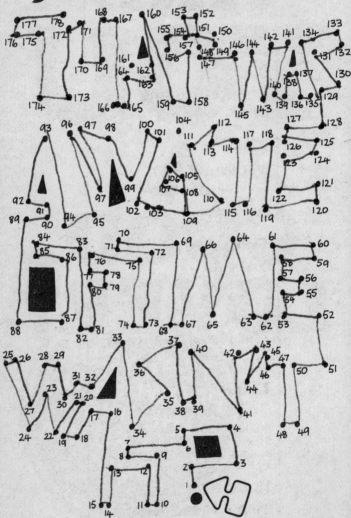

ARE YOU A GOOD LOVER?

TEST YOUR PROWESS ON THE IRISH KAMA SUTRA QUIZ

QUESTIONS FOR MEN

ONE

Do you make love to your wife . . .?
A)   Before a good sleep
B)   After a good sleep
✔C)   During a good sleep

TWO

How often do you make love to your wife . . .?
A)   Once a night
✔B)   Twice a night
C)   Bank Holiday Monday

THREE

Are you a . . . . . ?
A)   Bum man
B)   Breast man
C)   Leg man
✔D)   Coalman

FOUR

What is the capital city of Venezuela . . . . ?
A)   Stockholm
B)   Caracas
✔C)   Bournemouth
D)   Newport Pagnell

FIVE

What's your pet name for your wife when you're making love . . . .?
A)   Dumpling
B)   Honey Bum
C)   Mrs. O'Rourke
✔D)   Champion the Wonder Horse

SIX

Do you make love . . .?

A) With the light on
B) With the light off
✓C) Not wearing a light
D) Caracas

SEVEN

What do you enjoy your lover doing to you most . . .?

A) Tickling your tiddler
✓B) Gobbling your gonger
C) Nibbling your nobbler
D) Scratching your caracas

EIGHT

Who do you imagine you're in bed with when you're making love . . .?

A) Brigitte Bardot
✓B) Debbie Harry
C) Anna Ford
D) Ena Sharples
E) Miss Piggy
F) Les Dawson
G) The Blackwall Tunnel

QUESTIONS FOR WOMEN

ONE

What do you wear in bed . . .?
A) Nothing
B) A nightie
C) Thermal underwear
✓D) A diving suit
E) Cricket pads
F) Val Doonican's sweaters
G) All of the above

TWO

How many times have you been unfaithful to your partner . . .?
A) Never
B) Once every so often
C) Twice every so often
✓D) Only on weekdays ending in 'y'

THREE

Do you prefer it . . .?
A) From the back
B) From the front
C) From the side
D) Or are you perfectly satisfied with your new haircut?

FOUR

How far did you go on your first date . . .?
A) Necking
B) Groping
C) All the way
✓D) Aberdeen

FIVE

Which of the following inanimate objects excites you the most . . .?

A)   A banana

✓B)   A cucumber

C)   A hairdryer

D)   A Radio One disc jockey

SIX

Do you like it . . .?

A)   Up the rear

B)   Up the front

✓C)   Up the Hammers

SEVEN

Do you make love . . .?

A)   Only in bed

B)   Only under the bed

✓C)   Only on top of the wardrobe

D)   Only in Sainsbury's

EIGHT

Who do you imagine you're in bed with when you're making love . . .?

A)   Robert Redford

B)   Tom Jones

C)   Jack Jones

D)   Les Dawson

E)   Pinky and Perky

F)   Ena Sharples

✓G)   The Post Office Tower

TURN TO PAGE 106 AND SEE HOW WELL YOU'VE SCORED!!

ARE YOU FED UP WITH SEX ?

THE IRISH KAMA SUTRA HAS THIS NOVEL SUGGESTION FOR SOMETHING TO DO TO ALLEVIATE THE BOREDOM:

TEAR THIS PAGE INTO A THOUSAND PIECES AND THEN ATTEMPT TO STICK THEM BACK TOGETHER AGAIN WITH YOUR TONGUE.

MURFY'S TALE

The following true story is the tale of a man whose sex life was transformed by 'The Irish Kama Sutra'. We feel that we must warn you, the reader, that there is a certain passage in this story which could in all fairness be described as extremely dirty, and might easily cause offence to those of a puritanical disposition.

If, however, you are a foul-minded, dirty-thinking little runt, and want to skip the boring, narrative part, I might as well tell you that the extremely dirty bit occurs near the end of the tale. I can't actually tell you the page number, but if you rearrange the two digits 5 and 7 I think you'll probably stumble on it.

MURPHY'S TALE

Monday morning started as usual with the end of Sunday night.

Murphy opened the window to let the sun in, but it had already come in through the back door, scorched the room, and gone out again.

It was a typically hot August morning.

'What's it doing here in the middle of February?' thought Murphy.

He flicked through his diary. Monday, Tuesday, Wednesday, Thursday, Friday.

'It's going to be one of those weeks', Murphy decided.

He looked at the day's date. Monday February 47th.

'Ah! Leap Year'.

He read the entry for the day before.

'Dear Diary. Today is Sunday'

Then he read Saturday's entry.

'Dear Diary, Today is Saturday'

Then Friday's

'Dear Diary. Today is Wednesday'

That must have been an interesting day!

Murphy's empty diary reminded him that his sex life was disastrous. Six months since he'd had a date, and nearly a year since he'd had a banana. He tied a cigarette to a piece of rope and hauled it around the bedroom a few times. He always enjoyed the first drag of the day.

Murphy shuffled into the bathroom and looked at himself in the mirror. He noticed the red mark on his face from where he had burnt himself the previous week. Someone had phoned him while he was doing the ironing.

He examined the five o'clock shadow on his chin, then looked at his watch. Nine o'clock.
'Hell, my face has stopped', panicked Murphy.
'I must remember to wind it up in future'.
He heard Rover barking.
'Here, boy', he shouted.
Rover padded into the bathroom, clutching a brown envelope in his mouth, and still bleeding from where the postman had bitten him.
'Woof, woof', barked Rover.
'What a very talented cat Rover is', thought Murphy.
Murphy picked up the envelope, collected his newspaper, and then went into the kitchen to make his breakfast. He put the kettle on the cooker.

He took the eggs out of the fridge, put the newspaper in the toaster, and started reading a slice of bread. He got bored with the first slice so he went straight to the end of the loaf to find out that the crust did it. Murphy picked up his letter, and examined it with great excitement; he hadn't had a letter for months. Not since he'd received an invitation to his grandmother's funeral. He'd decided not to go because her funerals were always the same; held in some draughty old cemetery, and never enough booze. Murphy thought that this was probably another of his granny's invitations. She died approximately sixteen times a year, but then she was an extremely sick woman.

Just then the phone rang. Murphy picked it up.

'Is dat Cork double t'ree, double t'ree?' enquired a voice.

'No, dis is Cork treble t'ree t'ree' explained Murphy.

'Oh, Oi must have the wrong number. Sorry to disturb you.'

'Da'ts alright. I was answering der phone anyway'.

Murphy returned to his letter, and started to open it as he spread butter and marmalade onto his newspaper. He was right; it was an invitation. Not from his grandmother, though, but from a total stranger. The gilt-edged invitation dropped out of the envelope and onto the table. Murphy examined it quizzically, holding it up to the light.

Why could he not make head nor tail of it? Because it was in code? Because it was in a foreign language? Because it was in mirror writing? Or because Murphy couldn't read? Luckily, Rover the cat not only did a passable impression of a dog but was also literate. The invitation read as follows:

AN EXCLUSIVE INVITATION
TO READERS OF
THE IRISH KAMA SUTRA

You don't know us ... but we don't know you either.
Small world, in't it?

LORD O'REILLY
and
LADY O'REALLY

request the pleasure of your company at the

SEXUAL ADVENTURE OF
A LIFETIME!
A MASKED ORGY OF
UNBRIDLED
LUST & PERVERSION

to be held on March 17th
in the Grounds of the O'Reilly Estate
(or if wet in The Vicarage)

DRESS OPTIONAL

Wenches will be provided
but please bring a bottle of Guinness.
All Night Disco till 9.45 p.m.
Lavatories open till 10.30 p.m.
Whips Provided
Confessions heard and palms read by
Father Thanthiswedarenotgo

COME IF YOU CAN!   R.S.V.P.

Murphy couldn't believe his luck.
'I can't believe my luck', said Murphy.
There you are, I told you he couldn't believe his luck.

Murphy had consulted a map before leaving home, and decided to break his journey in a little, sleepy village called Cockwell. As he neared Cockwell, though, his journey was interrupted by a leprechaun jumping into his path. Now it is a well-known piece of Irish bull that when a leprechaun crosses your path, he must grant you two wishes. Luckily from the story's point of view, the leprechaun had heard this idle rumour and believed it. He asked Murphy what his first wish was to be. 'Oh bejasus . . . er . . .', stumbled Murphy. 'Well, sor, I think I'll choose a whisky bottle that never runs dry'.
At that very moment a whisky bottle magically appeared in Murphy's hand.
'Oh, Bejasus, thank you, sor'.
said Murphy, as he quickly unscrewed the top, took a long drink and examined the bottle. It was still completely full. Murphy was ecstatic.
'And what second wish would you be wanting?' asked the leprechaun.
'Oh, I'll have another one of these please.'

Murphy continued his journey looking forward intensely to the orgy at the O'Reilly estate and the extremely dirty bit of the story. As evening fell, Murphy arrived at the small village of Cockwell. He had once gone out with a girl from Cockwell called Mary Anne O'Danaghue. Many evenings they would spend romantically playing darts and getting rotten steaming drunk at the local inn. A charming tudor public house by the village green. How Mary Ann loved the Cockwell Inn. As Murphy wandered up the village High Street he saw an old drunk on his hands and knees, searching for something under the orange glow of a streetlight. 'What have you lost, my good man, that you search with such alacrity in the long grass under the pale glow of the orange street light?' inquired Murphy in his best Queen's English. 'Mind your own fxbg£Zm½bg business, you big queen!' replied the man.

'Can Oi be of assistance?' proffered Murphy.

'Oi've lost a coin. A twopenny coin. My only worldly possession.'

'I'll help you look for it', said Murphy.

After searching for two hours, Murphy asked,

'Are you sure you dropped it in dis precise spot?'

'No' replied the old man, 'Oi dropped it about a mile down der road, but the light's better here'.

'What a simple old man you are!' chuckled Murphy, and kicked him in the head

'You must take pity on me, sor. I am a poor drunken wretch who hasn't eaten for two years.'

'All roight', said Murphy. 'Here's what Oi'll do. In my cart Oi have a sack containing some potatoes. If you can guess how many there are in it, you can have both of them'

The old man agreed. He thought for a while.

'Mmmm. I know. T'ree!'

'No!' said Murphy. 'You're one out. There are seven!'

'Oh do let me have them' cried the wizened, decrepit, senile drunkard.

'Oi've led a sinful life. Having twenty women a night and drinking t'ree bottles of whisky a day for breakfast . . . and now Oi repent and cry out for help and food!'

'You've obviously lived a good life', said Murphy. 'And you seem to have survived your ill-spent years. How old are you, in fact?'

'Twenty five', replied the old man.

Murphy told the old man that he was on his way to the O'Reilly estate for a grand orgy.

'Ah, yes', said the old man. 'Dat must be der extremely dirty bit of dis story. Oi'm looking forward to it. Do you t'ink Oi'm going ter be in it?'

'Oi've no idea', replied Murphy. 'Oi don't like skipping straight to the end of a book when Oi'm the central character.'

So Murphy invited the old drunk to join him for a drink in the Cockwell Inn.

'You shall be rewarded in heaven for your kindness', blabbered the old man.

'You see, Oi am in fact none other than the Son of Man!'

'What?' cried Murphy.

'Dat's roight', continued the wino. 'I am Our Lord Himself'.

'Oi'm sorry, but Oi don't believe you', argued Murphy.

'You'll have to prove it'.

'Come with me' the old man said.

The two men walked into the public bar of the Cockwell Inn. The barman took one look at the old man, and said,

'Jesus Christ! Not you again'.

Murphy was overwhelmed. He immediately went down on his knees. (His contact lens had fallen out),

'Two pints of Guinness,' said Murphy to the landlord, a Mr. Robert O'Wass.

'Two pints of Guinness for me too' said the old man.
'I'm sorry, but I can't serve you yet, gentlemen', said the barman. 'There's still ten minutes to go before opening time'.
The two men were visibly disappointed. The barman continued, 'I'll tell you what, would you like a drink while you are waiting?'
'Dat's very kind of you' said Murphy. 'Oi'll have a whisky'
'Double?'
'Oh no', said Murphy. 'I couldn't manage a large one at the moment. Just a single'.
'Anything in it?'
'Yes', said Murphy, 'Another whisky'
'I'll have a pint of Guinness,' said the old man.
'I'm afraid we've run out of Guinness' replied the barman.
'Oi'll just have a half then' said the old man.
'Just a half! What sorta drink is that for an Irishman?' sneered the barman. 'Have a pint!'
'Oh, all right then' said the tramp. 'Oi'll have a pint'.
'One pint of Guinness coming up.'

The barman asked Murphy who he was and what he was doing in that part of the world.
'I'm on me way to the grand orgy at the O'Reilly estate', Murphy told him.
'Oh yes. The extremely dirty bit of the story. Am I in it?' asked the barman.
'I've no idea. I don't know how the story ends!' said Murphy.
'What a pity' sighed the barman, who smiled cannily, knowing that as soon as he'd got Murphy

out of his pub, he would skip a few pages and find out whether or not he was involved in the extremely dirty bit of the story.

And so a merry evening was begun. Murphy met some interesting characters in the Cockwell Inn. It was a very pleasant wood-panelled bar, with heads of deer and foxes sticking out from the wall.
'They must have been travelling at a fair pace when they hit the wall,' said one chap.

'You see the great red deer over there', said the barman. 'The one with those huge antlers. Well, that's the mad stag of Inniskillin. That beast killed my little brother Danny'.
'Was he a hunter then?' queried Murphy.
'No, he was sitting over there in the corner, having a drink and it fell off the wall and knocked him stone dead.'
Just at that moment a man walked into the bar holding a front door under his arm.
'Patrick, what the hell are you doing bringing your front door to the pub?'
'Well', explained Patrick. 'Oi've lost the key, see, so I can't lock the door. And I didn't want to be burgled. So I took the door off to keep it with me.'
Everyone agreed that this was prudent thinking on Paddy's part. But then Mick McFagan, Professor of Philosophy at the Sligo Institute of Tractor Maintenance remarked wisely.
'But how are you going to get in, Paddy?'
'Oh, don't worry about dat, Mick McFagan', replied Paddy. 'I've left all the windows open'.
There was a general murmur of admiration at the

rational and practical philosophical systems of Paddy and McFagan. And as the evening went on the more and more epistemological they got.

Murphy looked up and saw over the bar, in a glass box, the tail of a dog. Standing in front of the tail the barman told the sad tale behind the tail of the dog.
'When I first took over this pub, some twenty years ago now, the previous landlord left me a little puppy. I called it Carpenter, cause he was always doin' little odd jobs around the house . . . and if you kicked him hard enough he'd make a bolt for the door. He became a great companion to me. Truly my best friend. I never really got on with my wife; she didn't understand me, and was always scolding me. Yet little Carpenter didn't seem to mind when I peed against lamp posts and chewed the carpet. He really understood me. Every night I'd put on his lead, and he'd put on mine, and we'd go for a walk together. I'd chat to him about life and death, and he'd bark back at me as if to say, 'I don't understand a word you're saying'.
We got on so well. But death comes to us all, as you know, and a few years ago I died. But I have a good solicitor and a mean wife who didn't want to pay death duties, so I got out of it somehow. But, alas, my little doggy could not avoid the fatal knell . . . he died. Well, he was an insomniac dog so I had him put to sleep.
I couldn't stand the thought of being without him. So before he was buried I cut off his tail and put it in a box in the bar as a constant memento of my greatest friend. But my little doggy went up to Heaven, and when he got to the Pearly Gates, St. Peter said,

'Where's your tail, little doggy?'
My doggy told him.
'Go back and get it' said St. Peter. 'We can't let you come in here without your tail'.
And so, in the dead of night, the ghost of my little doggy came to visit me to ask for his tail back.
'So why is his tail still here?' asked Murphy.
The barman replied,
'It's a pub rule. I can't retail spirits after hours'.
Murphy sat dumbfounded at the poor punchline simply longing for the O'Reilly orgy and the extremely dirty bit of the story.

The following morning Murphy was up at the crack of dawn. An hour or so later he took his suitcase down from the wardrobe and packed his bags. Although, why he'd brought a caseful of brown paper bags remains a mystery.
Murphy left the Cockwell Inn, and continued on his journey.
He followed the Dublin Road for a few miles, then it shook him off down a side street. Murphy travelled on foot for the next ten miles, then he decided to travel on both feet so that he'd travel twice as quickly.
He suddenly found himself in a deserted, narrow lane.
The sky darkened menacingly; the wind blew fiercely; the trees quivered quiveringly Murphy was afraid, well aware that this area was notorious for attacks on unsuspecting travellers by cut-throat thieves.
As Murphy turned a corner he was stopped in his tracks by a masked man wearing a large black cape, clutching a revolver and riding a big black stallion.

'Scuse me. Do you know the way to the fancy dress party?' he asked.

Murphy shook his head and moved on . . . but not very far, because a huge unkempt Irishman suddenly jumped out from behind a bush. Murphy could tell that this one had a price on his head. (He'd just bought a new hat and had forgotten to take the label off.)

'Stand and deliver', he growled. 'Your money or your life.'

'American Express' said Murphy.

'That'll do nicely, sir', said the man, and moved on.

Murphy carried on until he stopped in front of a large wooden entrance to a mansion.

'I wonder what that's doing in the middle of the road?' thought Murphy, as he stepped past it, and continued on his way.

It wasn't long, though before our hero was standing in front of the imposing O'Reilly estate. He made his way to the front of the big house and knocked nervously on the door of solid oak. The door was opened by a liveried flunkey wearing a powdered wig, doublet and hose. He had just come in from watering the garden.

'Good evening, Mr. Murphy,' the man boomed. 'May I have your invitation'.

Murphy handed him the gilt-edged card.

'Thank's a lot', said the flunkey. 'I haven't got one, you see'. And with that he slammed the door in Murphy's face.

Fortunately Murphy had had the foresight to bring his copy of 'The Irish Kama Sutra' with him. He knocked again and showed the flunkey the book.

Having proved that he was a member of the Irish Kama Sutra Society, he was welcomed to the party.

Murphy walked into the Great Hall. He could not believe his eyes. Wherever he looked, there were beautiful, naked girls, licking their lips and eyeing him greedily. Best of all, he was the only man in the entire room. The door to the Great Hall swung shut, and was bolted from the outside. In the centre of the hall was a huge heated swimming pool filled with foam. The prettiest girl in the whole room was swaying provocatively in the middle of this pool, water dripping off her voluptuous body with bits of foam stuck tantalizingly to her.
'Come on in', she beckoned, 'We've been waiting for you for so long, Murphy'.
Seventy-nine nubile young girls quickly and efficiently stripped Murphy naked, and then everyone jumped into the pool, including our hero.

Right, here comes the extremely dirty bit . . . the bit you've all been waiting for. We suggest that you pause for a moment, pour yourself a large drink and a cold bath, then turn to the next page.

THE EXTREMELY DIRTY BIT

THE IRISH LIMERICK

That great verse form the Irish Limerick is more correctly called the Irish Tipperary because Edward O'Leer, who invented it, came from Tipperary. (His mother came from Longford, but that's another story). In the interests of culture, and without the financial assistance of the Arts Council, the *Irish Kama Sutra* now proudly presents some of O'Leer's most profound poetic gems.

The Creation by E. O'Leer
In the Garden of Eden lay Adam
Complacently stroking his madam,
   And loud was his mirth
   For on all of the earth
There were only two balls – and he had 'em.

Three Months Gone by E. O'Leer
There was a young lady from Thrace
Whose corsets no longer would lace.
   Her mother said, 'Nelly,
   There's more in your belly
Than ever went in through your face.'

A Religious Experience by E. O'Leer
There was an Irish monk in Siberia
Whose existence grew steadily drearier,
   Till he broke from his cell
   With a hell of a yell
And eloped with the Mother Superior.

Amadeus by E. O'Leer
(Sometimes attributed to L. O'Carroll)
As Mozart composed a sonata
The maid bent to fasten her garter.
  Without delay
  He started to play
Un poco piu appasionata.

Down Memory Lane by E. O'Leer
A girl who would not be disgraced
Would flee from all lovers in haste.
  It all went quite well
  Till one day she fell . . .
She sometimes still dreams that she's chaste.

The End by E. O'Leer
There was a most finicky lass
Who always wore knickers of brass.
  When they asked, 'Don't they chafe?'
  She said, 'Yes, but I'm safe
From pinches and pins in the – grass.'

IRISH KAMA SUTRA CRYPTIC
CROSSWORD

CLUES
Across.
1. The first letter of the English alphabet. (1)
(Anagram)

Down.
1. The indefinite article. See 1. across.

KEY:
Across
1. Beethoven

Down
1. Isle of Wight.

IRISH KAMA SUTRA EVEN MORE CRYPTIC CROSSWORD

CLUES

Across

1.   Perhaps not in dictionary, not quite, doubtlessly while on vacation in Shakespearean sauna, initially, but not for young ladies. Interesting! (12 & 7)

Answer in next year's edition.

AN IRISH CROSSWORD PUZZLE

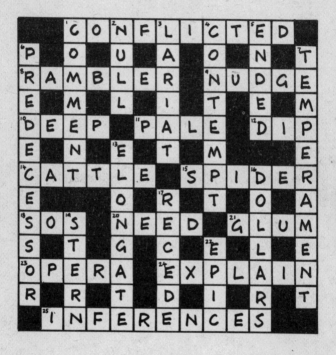

CLUES

Across.

1.

8.

9.

10.

11.

12.

14.

15.

18.

20. WANT.

21.

23.

24.

25.

Down.

1.

2.

3.

4.

5.

6.

7.

13.

16.

17.

19.

22.

AN IRISH LETTER

One of our readers sent us this kind letter, and we'd like to share it with you.

Dear Irish Kama Sutra Editors,

WOW!!! Am I glad I bought your book!!! I've just been on holiday in Donegal, and, BOY, did I get a lot of use out of it!
(And out of the book as well.) Ouch!
My little joke there!!

Seriously though, Donegal's a truly amazing place! The girls there are the prettiest I have ever seen. And wherever you go, they offer to make mad passionate love to you - in the cinema, in the supermarket, wherever.

I had a fantastic holiday, and made full use of your book's advice!!!
Thanks a lot, Irish Kama Sutra!!!

Must go now. I'm off to book my holiday for next year at the travel agent's. Where am I going??? You guessed it!! DONEGAL!
Bye!!!

Best wishes,

Patrick O'Donegal

Patrick O'Donegal
Chairman
Irish Tourist Board

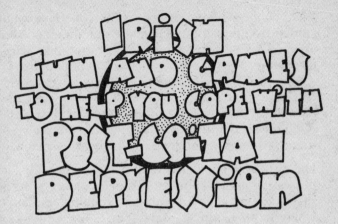

IRISH FUN AND GAMES TO HELP YOU COPE WITH POST-COITAL DEPRESSION

IRISH JOKES

Did you hear about the Irishman who put a clean pair of socks on every day and by the end of the week he couldn't get his shoes on?

Did you hear about the Irish Show Jumper who fractured his skull jumping against the clock?

Did you hear about the Irish jellyfish?
It set.

Did you hear about the little Irish lass who tried to put toilet water behind her ears but the seat kept falling on her head?

Did you hear about the Irishman who moved his house twenty feet to take up the slack in his washing line?

Did you hear about the Irishman who thought that Hertz Van Rental was a Dutch footballer?

Did you hear about the Irish prostitutes who picketed the 'Do It Yourself' Exhibition?

Did you hear about the two Irish fishermen who landed twenty fish in their first two minutes on the water? One says to the other. 'This is a great place for fishing. We'll have to row back here tomorrow'. 'Good idea', says the other one, 'But we'll never find this exact spot again!' 'Well, we'll have to mark the place somehow', says the other, 'I know, I'll draw an X on the side of the boat'. 'That's no good', says his friend, 'we might not get the same boat tomorrow.'

Did you hear about the Irish hooligan arrested for possessing a flick-hammer. His mate was carrying a razor, but he got off because he couldn't find anywhere to plug it in.

Did you hear about the Irish Jellyfish that set?
Yes, I heard that on the previous page, actually.
Oh, sorry.

IRISH PATIENCE

Introducing a new game of patience that's guaranteed to lift you when you're down. Cut out the card; shuffle, deal and play. This game will keep you happy for years.

Dear Meg...

The chapter in which the famous Irish sexologist, Dr. Kerry Patrick O'Connell, or Meg as we call him here, lends a knowing eye, a sympathetic ear, and a rather encouraging ankle to your personal, emotional and sexual problems.

Dear Meg,
I'm very worried about the size of my shillelagh. My girlfriend laughs at it when I show her. It's just under 1½ inches long and ½ an inch wide . . . And it's been swollen up like that for weeks.
Yours,
Joe Ballyvaghan.

Meg Answers: That's a ridiculously puerile and ancient joke, Joe. You should be ashamed of it.

Dear Meg,
That's just what my girlfriend says when I take my trousers off.
Yours,
Joe Ballyvaghan

Dear Meg,
My husband Paddy is a compulsive gambler. He spends and loses all his money on the horses. What should I do to help him?
Yours,
Louise.

Meg Answers: Dear Louise, why don't you study form? Yours, Meg.

Dear Meg,
My wife's run off with the gas man. What should I do?
Yours,
Mike Arnold.

Meg Answers: Dear Mike, I should go electric. Yours, Meg.

Dear Meg,
I think my husband Jamie is having an affair, but I don't know who she is. Can you help.
Yours,
Julie Hulvil of Lewisham.

Meg Answers: Dear Julie, I can certainly help. Her name is Helen Jessy Rhone and she lives in Swiss Cottage. Yours, Meg.

Dear Meg,
It's not me. I've never met Jamie.
Yours,
Helen Jessy Rhone

Meg Answers: Dear Julie and Helen, In that case, it's Andrea the barmaid. Yours. Meg.

Dear Meg,
I took your advice and went electric. I got back with the wife as well, but our first night together was a disaster. She went up in a puff of blue smoke. Perhaps I shouldn't have gone electric.
Yours,
Mike Arnold.

Dear Meg,
I am a very large industrial city, and I'm frightened of getting too big.
Yours,
Worried Manchester.

Dear Meg,
My O'Toole is twelve inches long, but I don't use it as a rule.
Yours,
Dr. Christopher Neightley.

Dear Meg,
A lot of girls have told me that they like a good ten inches, but I'm not folding mine in half for anybody.
Yours,
Peter Fincham.

Meg Answers:
How many times do I have to tell you men that size is not important. What matters is how big it is.
Yours,
Meg.

IRISH
ADDRESS
BOOK

A
B
C
D
E
F
G
H
I
J
K
L
M
N
O
P
Q
R
S
T
U
V
W
X
Y
Z

The Junior Kama Sutra

SEX EDUCATION FOR TEACHERS

(Warning: This article is not fit for children.)

In today's permissive society it's very important that teachers have a clear knowledge and understanding of the facts of life. They must be taught at an early age about the birds and bees. (Although it's still not clear why a bird should want to have it off with a bee.) It's vital that young teachers aren't misled by old wives' tales. So don't tell them any tales about old wives. Most teachers think that babies are brought by a stork. This of course is not true. Babies are made by mummies and daddies.

Inside mummy there is a little blob of stuff:

● ← A LITTLE BLOB OF STUFF

Inside daddy there is a little blob of stuff:

● ← ANOTHER BLOB OF STUFF

This last blob
grows a little
bit:

● ← A SLIGHTLY BIGGER BLOB OF STUFF

When these two little blobs of stuff come together they make a slightly bigger blob of stuff:

And then a bit more:

And then a bit more:

And a bit more:

And then it grows into a gooseberry bush and you find the baby underneath it one morning.

A SONNET

Mine eyes and heart are at mortal war,
How to divide the conquest of thy sight;
Mine eye my heart thy picture's sight would bar,
My heart mine eye the freedom of that right.
My heart doth plead that thou in him dost lie,
A closet never pierced with crystal eyes,
But the defendant doth that plea deny,
And says in him thy fair appearance lies.
To 'cide this title is impannelled
A quest of thoughts, all tenants to the heart;
And by their verdict is determined
The clear eye's moiety and the dear heart's part;
    As thus; mine eye's due is thine outward part,
    And my heart's right thine inward love of heart.'

AUTHORS NOTE

The authors of 'The Irish Kama Sutra' would like to say how sorry they are about the opposite page. It's like this, you see. We went into the publishers one day, and the editor said, 'I think it'd be really nice if the Irish Kama Sutra had a poem in it'. So we thought OK, good idea . . . one of those ditties that starts 'T'was on the good ship Venus', something like that. Then she suggested Shakespeare. Well, what can you do? You don't want to appear ignorant, do you? So we said OK.

Hence, the preceding page. Anyway, look, we want you to know that we're really, really, really sorry about it, and hope it doesn't mar your judgement of the otherwise extremely high literary standard of this unique publication.

USEFUL IRISH PROVERBS

Too many cooks spoil the broth. Don't put them in it in the first place.

Don't carry coals to Newcastle. Send them by post.

Don't count your chickens before you've left the Freezer Centre unseen by the store detective.

You can lead a horse to water but you can't solve Europe's economic problems.

If at first you don't succeed, kill the spider.

The IRISH KAMA SUTRA

MALE PLEASURE GRAPH

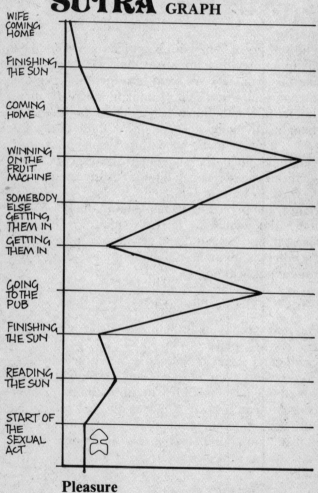

- WIFE COMING HOME
- FINISHING THE SUN
- COMING HOME
- WINNING ON THE FRUIT MACHINE
- SOMEBODY ELSE GETTING THEM IN
- GETTING THEM IN
- GOING TO THE PUB
- FINISHING THE SUN
- READING THE SUN
- START OF THE SEXUAL ACT

Pleasure

The IRISH KAMA SUTRA

FEMALE PLEASURE GRAPH

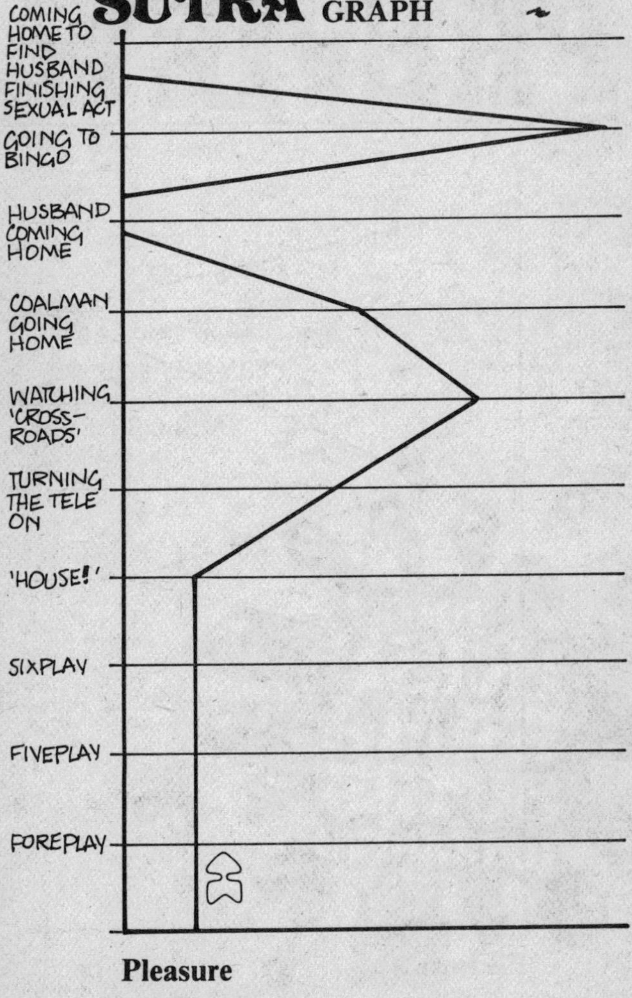
COMING HOME TO FIND HUSBAND FINISHING SEXUAL ACT
GOING TO BINGO
HUSBAND COMING HOME
COALMAN GOING HOME
WATCHING 'CROSS-ROADS'
TURNING THE TELE ON
'HOUSE!'
SIXPLAY
FIVEPLAY
FOREPLAY
Pleasure

P.T.O.

FILM PREVIEW

Our roving reporter
Sheila Stuffall, reports on
her sneak previews of films
of a sexual nature that are
about to come to Ireland. This
week . . . A BLOB OF INK

an IRISH KAMA SUTRA exclusive

Hi there, film goers!
You've had 'The Bitch'
(You've read the book, you've seen the movie).
You've had 'The Stud'
(You've read the book, you've seen the movie).
You've had 'The World is full of Married Men'.
(You've read the book, you've seen the movie).
And now . . . about to hit your screens is Jackie
O'Goblins' latest film . . . 'A BLOB OF INK'.

Yes, film goers, a great new picture based on the book by Jackie O'Goblins and of course starring Jackie's celebrated aunt June O'Goblins, and introducing her nice niece, Jane O'Goblins plus, of course, a great supporting cast of her brother, Canon John O'Goblins, her step-brother Tom O'Goblins her German butler, Johann, her uncle Bruno, her cousins Phil and Maxine, her doctor, Chris Neightley, Mrs. Biddlecombe, the lady from the Women's Institute, some people she once met at a party in Brighton, a hundred people she once saw on a train going to Northampton, her dog, Spike, her dog's elder sister, Joan, Joan's favourite bone, Basil, her Spanish boyfriend Rafael, her vacuum cleaner, her yoyo, all her shoes.

Yes, June O'Goblins is stupendous in 'A Blob of Ink' . . . the gripping story of an ageing woman and her lonely, desperate struggle to take her clothes off in front of an innocent and unsuspecting group of film cameramen.

'A BLOB OF INK' . . . THE MOST EXCITING THING YET TO COME FROM THE PEN OF JACKIE O'GOBLINS.

Other films not to be missed:
'Black Emmanuelle Two Goes Yellow'
The story of a beautiful girl's fight with hepatitis.
'Carry on Camping'
The hilarious story of the demise of British cinema.

A PRE-RECORDED MESSAGE FOR AVID CINEMA-GOERS

This is the Odeon Theatre, Cork, with details of today's programmes. At studios one, two, three, four and all even numbers up to one hundred and forty we will be showing 'Emmanuelle'. This is an 'X' certificate film with people in it.

The programme starts at 6 p.m. We will first be showing that annoyingly long cigarette advert set in Zululand, followed by the totally incomprehensible film, featuring lizards and helicopters, which is pretty to look at but has sweet F.A. to do with Benson and Hedges.

Having whet your appetite for a fag you will then start to light up, just as we remind you that you are sitting in the cinema's 'NO SMOKING' sector. At 6.30 two OAPs will start talking very loudly behind you, whilst a man wearing a busby will take the seat in front of you.

At eight o'clock a bunch of zombies will come round being gratuitously rude to you and selling you warm ice cream and plastic flavoured orange juice. Next, we will relax you, with a charming short film about two young lovers, who have a casual drink, drive away into the sunset together, write a car off, and suffer multiple lacerations and head wounds.

At this point we advise you to visit the lavatory because once the film starts these will be locked. REMEMBER – an hour from now you'll wish you'd had one.

On returning to your seat, we will torture your social conscience with a tragic comic film appeal on behalf of the Variety Club of Great Britain. Following this, the zombies will return, waggling collection boxes at you until you agree to part with your bus fare home. Should you want to know when the film starts, please ring this entirely different number – 2456801. The Odeon Theatre, Cork, would like to thank you for this four minute call on behalf of the Post Office.

COME BACK SOON.

PERSONAL COLUMN

One more Aquarian, non-smoking, macrobiotic, Ginseng drinking, animal loving bisexual wanted to join Overland trip to Kafmandu in a Morris Minor. Box 231.

MICHAEL Tarot. Professional clairvoyant and mind reader. Don't ring him, he'll ring you.

OLD man seeks young children (preferably boys) to share flat in Earls Court for a limited period. Box 251.

OLD/Young Man/Woman seeks skilled, unscrupulous surgeon. Box 231.

Answers

Question One
If you make love before a good sleep you get ten points
If you make love after a good sleep you get twenty points
And if you make love during a good sleep you get arrested.

Question Two
Five points for Bank Holiday Monday, but no points if it was 'Bank Holiday Monday, August 1938'.

Question Three
Bum man, Breast man, and Leg man all get ten points. If your answer was Coal man you get twenty points for having the honesty to admit that you find bits of coal sexually arousing.

Question Four
Ten points for Caracas, and five consolation points for Newport Pagnell since the Mayor of Newport Pagnell is a personal friend.

Question Five
Ten points for C if your name is Mr. O'Rourke.
(Ten points for D) only if your wife has the habit of running through the streets like a streak of lightning flashing through the sky. Give extra points if she has a cowboy on her back.

Question Six	Two points for everything if you told the truth. Nothing if you didn't.
Question Seven	
Question Eight	

Question One
1,000 points for everything. Actually, I'm not really in charge of the points. I'm the author of the book next door. Your man's in the boozer. He's gone for a quick one. He'll go mad when he gets back!

Question Two
Right. I'm back from the pub. Ignore that last question, please, ladies. Ten points if you've been unfaithful to your husband twice, but no points if that 'twice' was once with the milkman and once with the Household Cavalry.

Question Three
Ten points to the writers for clever, sexual innuendo.

Question Four
Ten points for Aberdeen. They need all the help they can get.

Question Five
Ten points for A, B or C but minus ten points for D. A radio one disc jockey – you pervert, you!

Question Six
Ten points for spotting the reference to West Ham United Football Club, Winners of the 1980 F.A. Cup (Well done, boys.)

Question Seven
Ten points for D. because everything in Sainsbury's is clean and fresh.

Question Eight
Ten points for everything, and it's back to the pub for me, I think.

Index

FIND THE PAGE YOU WANT

For quick and easy access to the page you want we have included this comprehensive index.

WHAT PEOPLE HAVE SAID ABOUT
'THE IRISH KAMA SUTRA'

'A gripping book. I couldn't put it down.'
>(Chairman of the Irish Glue Manufacturers
>Association)

'A stunning intellectual achievement. On a par only with Proust's "A La recherche du temps Perdu" and BBC 1's "Are you Being Served"
>(Samuel Buckett)

'The Irish Kama Sutra' is great and what's more . . .'
>(The Bachelors)

'Scuse us. But have you seen The Bachelors anywhere?'
>(The Unmarried Mothers)

'. . . Sorry, but we're going to have to go'
>(The Bachelors)

'You thought you were reading "The Irish Kama Sutra" but tonight, Albert Smith of Camden Town, This Is Your Life.'
>(Eamonn Andrews)

'W . . . w . . . w . . . w . . . w . . . w . . . w
>(Chairman of the Irish Board of Speech Therapists)

'I only read half of it'
>(Moshe Dayan)

'A sophisticated discourse on the sexual worries and inherent fears that face all members of today's society'
>(Eddie O'Waring)

'I'm convinced that it's a major contribution to road safety'
>(Sir Robert Mark)

OTHER BOOKS BY THE SAME AUTHORS

'THE STORY OF O'
A blow by blow account of the story of O (the unfinished
Irishman)

'NODDY GETS HIS OATS'
An adaptation of the Enid Blyton story in which Noddy buys
some porridge.

'BIG EARS GETS HIS OATS'
An adaptation of the Enid Blyton story in which Big Ears humps
Edna the Tea-Lady.

BIBLIOGRAPHY
The authors acknowledge their gratitude to the following
sources of reference:
'The Indian Kama Sutra'
'The Misprint' by Harold Punter
'Joy of Sex', 'More Joy of Sex', 'Getting Bored with Sex', and
'Oh, hell You Don't Want To Do It Again, Do You?'

THE OTHER END